T0193367

A Doctrine On
The Christian Life

VOLUME II

Dr. John Thomas Wylie

authorHOUSE®

AuthorHouse™
1663 Liberty Drive
Bloomington, IN 47403
www.authorhouse.com
Phone: 1 (800) 839-8640

Published by AuthorHouse 12/13/2019

ISBN: 978-1-7283-3977-1 (sc)
ISBN: 978-1-7283-3976-4 (e)

Print information available on the last page.

Scripture quotations marked KJV are from the Holy Bible, King James Version
(Authorized Version). First published in 1611. Quoted from the KJV Classic
Reference Bible, Copyright © 1983 by The Zondervan Corporation.

Scripture quotations marked RSV are taken from the Revised
Standard Version of the Bible, copyright © 1946, 1952, 1971 by
the Division of Christian Education of the National Council of
the Churches of Christ in the USA. Used by permission.

American Standard Version (ASV)
Public Domain

This book is printed on acid-free paper.

Contents

Introduction

In this publication, "A Doctrine On The Christian Life," I planned to cover the field of Christian Doctrine. I perceive the treatment is lacking. The idea of the subject blocks ampleness. Who could give a satisfactory treatment to such a teaching or doctrine? One ventures the supposition that the greater part of the adjustments in religious philosophy (Christian Theology) are the correct way.

Men are turning their contemplations toward the need and the reality of disclosure, of man's wrongdoing (sin) and vulnerability, of both the individual and social disappointment of man without God, of the ampleness of God's grace for man's need, and of the sureness of Jesus Christ and his saving work for mankind's history.

Man does not live by bread alone. It is more critical that man have something to live for than that he have something to live on; and existence without God isn't genuine life. Today, Modern man needs to confront that reality and acknowledge it.

Reverend Dr. John Thomas Wylie

Chapter One

The Christian's Mission And Work

WHAT WE ARE CONCERNED with here is simply the consideration of some of the fundamentals principles of Christian Life, especially when it is viewed as a life of redemption.

The Development Of The New Life

The primary thing we specified is the Christian's main goal is to work out and epitomize in his every day exercises the existence embedded in his heart when he (or she) becomes a Christian. This life looks for encapsulation and articulation. This is communicated from numerous points of view in the New Testament. The Christian is said to take after Jesus Christ (Mark 1:16 ff.; 2:14). He is a follower; that is, a student in the school of Jesus Christ (Matt. 28:19).

The Spirit of Christ is in him and he is driven by the Spirit (Rom. 8:9 ff., 14). the Spirit of Christ lives in him (Gal. 2:20) and he endeavors to convey each idea into subjection to Christ (II Cor. 10:5). He is to work out his salvation, since it is God that works in him to will and to do (Phil. 2:12-13).

We don't intend to state that the Christian life is just the encapsulation of some rule of awesome life embedded a the season of recovery which lives on freely of further support from the divine presence. God keeps on working in us, as these references appear. He keeps on stimulating in us and through us, and our main goal is to work diligently as far as possible what God works in us in the way of willing and doing.

That is an extensive articulation that Paul makes when he says to the Philippians that they should work out their own particular salvation with fear and trembling (Phil. 2:12). The word deciphered "work out" intends to work out to certainty, to convey to fruition. Paul does not mean, that one can work out his salvation without God. He doesn't intend to state that God started the procedure and now turn it over to man to wrap up.

The thinking is very unique in relation to that. Paul gives as the explanation behind his appeal that is God that works in us, both to will and to do. The accentuation is on the way that God works in us.

God works; he works in us; he works both to start (to will) and to finish (to do). It's anything but a co-agent exertion as in God conveys one end of the heap and man the other, functioning as equivalents.

The Apostle never would have admonished his readers to work with fear and trembling in the event that he had thought of the issue in that mold.

Paul does not talk here in the soul of an advanced, independent man, standing erect, with extended chest, opposing the universe and flaunting that he is the commander of his own spirit. He talks as a Jew respectfully bowing within the sight of the Lord of the universe, aware of his own creatureliness and corruption. Be that as it may, he is cognizant that the Lord of the universe as sacred and generous is managing him for his salvation.

He is a similar Paul who demanded that man gets salvation by confidence and that he doesn't accomplish it by works. God starts and God invigorates to finish the undertaking. However, the confidence by which man gets salvation is a confidence that complies. Paul had recently urged them to comply. He has quite recently held up Jesus Christ as the immense case of submission and as the colossal case of commendation as the consequence of dutifulness. Presently he asks them to have the same effectively respectful confidence.

They will work out to articulation in their lives what God works in them by the power of his Spirit. Awe must come to articulation. Confidence must take shape in character and life. Supernaturally embedded driving forces must be conveyed to fulfillment in fixity of character and Christian administration. Generally the perfect aim comes up short of finish acknowledgment. In this working out of our salvation, we discover consolation in the way that God attempts to will, as well as to do.

He empowers in the entirety of our goals and our strivings. In any case, his motivation isn't understood aside from as we respect him and work out to articulation in life what he works in us.

What we have been stating implies that the Christian is to carry on with his life on a redemptive premise. he is to recollect that he is a man reclaimed. He is likewise to recollect that his individual man is one for whom Christ passed on. This was highest in Paul's mind when he thought of his individual man.,

Paul would not energetically put a hindrance in the method for the weakest sibling. The thing that made him so watchful was the acknowledgment that the powerless sibling was on for whom Jesus Christ kicked the bucket. To sin against him was to sin against Jesus Christ (I Cor. 8:11-13 KJV).

Bring Others To Know And Serve Jesus Christ

The Christian's main goal, in another phase of it, is to carry others into saving relations with Jesus Christ and build up the Christ life in them. Each Christian ought to be an evangelist, an envoy of the "Good news." In this sense each Christian ought to be a minister. This is the unconstrained motivation of the new life in us-to convey another person to know Jesus Christ and appreciate the immense gift that he gives.

Our central goal is to shoulder observer to Jesus Christ from Jerusalem to the furthest piece of the earth. Any type of Christianity that does not have throbbing through it a powerful preacher and evangelistic motivation is a deteriorate shape. Furthermore, the Christian's central goal is to do everything he can to build up the Christ life in others after they have been carried into saving relations with him.

There are the individuals who look on such evangelistic and preacher exertion as an audacity. They clearly consider Christianity as being on indistinguishable premise from different frameworks that men have developed or found and view it as having about as much claim on the lives of men as these different frameworks.

On the off chance that that is everything to Christianity, they are right. On the off chance that Jesus Christ is to be sectioned with the immense thinkers and religious pioneers of humanity, at that point it is an insolence for his believers to ask and expect that all men wherever will recognize him as Savior and Lord to the rejection of every single other.

Then again, in the event that he is the thing that we have asserted for him, what we trust he guaranteed for himself, and what he has ended up being by what he has improved the situation men; all things considered no man can truly know him without having a consuming power, deep yearning that every single other man should know him. All things considered, the message about him and his saving power is really the gospel-the main gospel for lost and demolished men.

For one who knows him to decline to make him known is injustice to him and foul play to the individuals who are subject to us for a learning of that gospel. Missions and evangelism, in this manner, are not accidental or optional in the Christian life; they are of the specific substance of Christianity. Furthermore, any type of supposed Christianity that does not hone the spread of the gospel among men along these lines substantiates itself false in its claim.

Apply Christianity To All Of Life

The Christian's main goal is to do all the good he can in each domain of life. He is to look to make regnant the will of God in the entire degree of human life and society. There are those today who set over against each other evangelistic exertion and social administration. They would stigmatize one for the other. The individuals who underscore evangelism and criticize social administration assume that anything with the exception of direct religious work is skeptical.

Each great work is religious if finished with a rationale to praise God. There is no contention between serving God and helping men. Unquestionably the Christ who mended the collections of men and played out a supernatural occurrence to bolster the hungry huge crowds does not speak to a God who is disappointed with anything that improves this world a place in which to live.

The sort of devotion that believes that the main capacity of religion is to make a man pull back into some religious community and save his own soul and let the world go to the devil-that kind of devotion has a place with the medieval times, in the event that it has a place, anyplace. Nor is it the main capacity of Christianity to save souls of men from hellfire in the following life; they should be made noble in each connection of life.

The recovery of the individual and the recovery of society ought to never be set over against each other as contradictory things; it's anything but an issue of one to the rejection of the other. They are somewhat two things that are commonly reliant. The best way to redeem society is through the redeeming of the individual units of society. Furthermore, the main power that can redeem the individual is the good news of Jesus Christ.

Nor has the gospel done its full work in the life of the individual except if he is made right in each connection of life. The gospel makes a man live right on the planet, not pulled back from the world. Jesus Christ trained his disciples to implore that God's kingdom may come and God's will be done on earth as it is in heaven (Matt. 6:10 KJV).

These are the individuals who dissent that it is except if to endeavor to make this world a decent place in which to live. This world, they say, is a fallen world and can't be redeemed. It is futile to attempt.

Then again, there has been a sure kind of American religious felt that has been unduly hopeful in its pondered human culture. It assumed that basically human instinct was good, and that with a little exertion a state of society could before long be achieved that would be relatively good. At any rate some religious leaders put the accentuation at the wrong place.

They accentuate changing social conditions as opposed to redeeming men. They said our first undertaking is to change conditions; great conditions will make good men.

This accentuation wasn't right. This is a fallen world. There is some fact in the possibility that good conditions make good men. However, generally it is the other way. Good men make good conditions as opposed to good conditions making good men. Men are impacted by their condition; it lies in them. They are conceited and evil. They should be changed within, and only the power of God can do that.

In any case, this does not legitimize any Christian in accepting the mentality of saying that the world is bad to the point that there is no hope about it; that Christianity was never proposed to save the world yet just a couple from the mass of the fallen race; and that we should try to save these and let the world go on its approach to destruction, perdition.

The protest is made that detestable can't be annihilated from our reality and that there is no utilization to attempt. That is to some degree genuine. Indeed, this author would confirm it to be valid. The New Testament appears to be wherever to expect that detestable will continue to the end. Only at the last culmination will there be an entire partition of the good from the evil (detachment of the wheat from the tares) and finish triumph over wickedness. Jesus Christ appears to suggest this in the story of the tares (Matt. 13:24ff.) and in the illustration of the dragnet (Matt. 13:47 ff.).

To one raising this protest there is a reasonable and positive answer; to be specific, that there is a lot of distinction between wanting to make the world impeccable and attempting to improve it. Standard Protestant religious philosophy has held that no human individual could acquire flawlessness in this life; yet it has additionally held that there was the likelihood of inconclusive change for any Christian in this life.

Jesus Christ himself encouraged that the ideal character of God was to be our optimal (Matt. 5:48 KJV). Toward that perfect we are to endeavor.

Be that as it may, Jesus realizes that nobody of could completely acquire that perfect in this life. Be that as it may, he obviously implied for us to consider the perfect important and endeavor toward it as long as we live in this world.

Neither the human individual nor human culture is perfectible; however both can be improved by the grace of God. What's more, he is a poor Christian who does not advocate taking care of the shades of malice of life and really attempt to take care of them. Indeed, even the man who questions most strenuously to what is call the "social gospel" will work energetically to confine the intensity of a solid shrewdness like the alcohol and drug activity.

Jesus considered his disciples the salt of the earth and the light of the world (Matt. 5:13-14 KJV). They can be utilized for the profound salvation and unequivocal change of a few men. However, it is additionally evident that Christian people can be a raising impact in human culture and raise the ethical norms of a network or country should be possible for the entire world.

Jesus himself talks about the kingdom of heaven as a raising power on the planet (Matt. 13:33 ASV). He is additionally spoken to as advising his disciples to make disciples everything being equal. We are to go the extent that we can toward Christianizing all the world.

Chapter Two

Providence The Doctrine Stated

IT IS AN ESSENTIAL factor in the Christian view, that the world be considered as a providential order. By provision that God is working out a purpose in the life of man.

Faith on the planet as a providential request is associated with the Christian faith in the identity of God, in the teaching of creation and in the connection of God to the world and to man. Particularly is it associated with the Christian principle of recovery and in the Christian's understanding of salvation and fellowship with God in Christ.

One will probably put stock in fortune that he has faith in an personal God who is great and in the meantime omniscient and omnipotent, and who made and maintains all things. Assuming, besides, one trusts that this God isn't just the Creator and Sustainer of all things, but at the same time is the Redeemer God uncovered in Jesus Christ, who by the power of his grace looks for sinful men and draws them into fellowship with himself, at that point faith in provision turns into a conviction.

One can't trust in such a God as uncovered to us in the Old and New Testament Scriptures and in the redemptive work of Jesus Christ and not likewise trust that this God is working out some awesome and great purpose in the life of mankind.

It is sure that Jesus Christ and the writers of the New Testament had believed in such providential care over the lives of God's children.

Objections To The Doctrine

Many individuals, in any case, would deny that the world is a providential order. They hold that there are sure things in life that make it difficult to have faith in any divine purpose that we can perceive or know. There are numerous other people who are suspicious in regards to the issue, and numerous others, while believing in some broad path in divine provision, are significantly puzzled and regularly troubled about he matter.

The explanations behind this distrust and dissent may be summed up general as three. These are interwoven and closely related.

Objection Based On The Mechanical View Of The Universe

This view holds that the world in the entirety of its stages is administered by law; that normal law is settled and constant; and that there is to be discovered no more profound significance in life than such law communicates; that is, no importance at all in the genuine feeling of that term. Man himself is just the result of mechanical and organic powers and is just the most noteworthy sign of such power.

This view has been extraordinarily best in class and strengthened by the exceptional progress of science and the logical perspective of things in our cutting edge world. By the utilization of the learning acquired in logical examination, we have gotten the machine age. We have been so fruitful in designing and creating hardware that in the psyches of numerous the machine increasingly poses a threat than the man that made it. Man made the machine, and now the machine debilitates to eat up the man that made it.

In reply to this view, we should seriously mull over the issue, first, as to its bearing on our idea of man, and next as to our idea of God.

As to man, we should recall that man is more prominent than any science. Nature never gave us an art of anything. In the event that perpetual law spoke the last word, we would have no science. Science is the result of the psyche of man, and man is more noteworthy than any science that he has delivered.

Man creates the diverse sciences by his free, intentional examination of characteristic marvels. Man researches the actualities of nature, finds the relations of these certainties among themselves, and states these relations in what we term common law. In any case, the psyche of man that finds these actualities and follows their relations is more prominent than the realities found. Additionally, man is deliberate and free in his investigations of nature and her miracles.

With regards to the machine, man is more prominent than the machine that he makes and employments. Machines truly do no work. Man takes every necessary step, utilizing the machine as an apparatus. At the point when an agriculturist gathers a yield of grain with a cutting edge collector, it is extremely the rancher who reaps the product as really as when the antiquated agriculturist gathered the harvest as genuinely as when the old grass shearer at any point collected a field of grain. At the point when a calculator gives you the whole of a long queue of figures, it was the brain of man that did all the reasoning for the situation; the machine did none.

The advancement of science and development (invention), the tremendous measure of work done by present day hardware-this is a declaration, not that we live in a universe of mechanical need, yet rather that we live in a world in which mind is better than things and in which reason controls the huge apparatus that insight has created. Man is better than things and to law.

So far as God is concerned, law is God's technique for working. The world isn't administered by law; it is represented by law. Natural law isn't a force. Natural law is the announcement of a strategy as indicated by with some power works. An announcement of the law does not characterize the idea of the power at work; it just expresses the strategy as per which it works. God runs the world; natural law is his technique for working.

Nor is natural law fundamentally perpetual. In the event that the power back of the world and working in and through the world is in its definitive nature individual, at that point there is no inalienable motivation behind why it probably won't fluctuate from the standard technique and rise above on occasion the strategy for normal law.

Nor is there any explanation behind denying that this power is purposive or big-hearted essentially in light of the fact that it works in normal ways. In actuality, this very consistency may itself be confirmation of a kind reason. Neither God nor man could do a kindhearted reason in a world that worked by possibility.

On the off chance that the sun ascended in the east one day and in the west the following; on the off chance that one year it was warm in the mid year and cool in the winter and one more year the issue was switched; in the event that one day lying debased a man's character and the following day praised it; in such an upside down world it is hard to perceive how any great purposes could be worked out.

The regularities of nature and of the ethical world don't militate against the possibility that God is grinding away on the planet. To a man who has confidence in God these things rather talk about the steadiness of God's motivation; the regularities of the world's task discuss the loyalty of God in doing his motivation on the planet.

Objection To The Doctrine Of Divine Providence Based On the Exaltation Of Man

A few men would concur with what we have been saying in regards to men's predominance over nature and hardware, yet would not remember him as subordinate to God and his purposes. We are not talking now of the kind of imagined that commends man yet makes him subservient to God. This kind humanism perceives God and would demand that faith in God exalts man.

Yet, there is a sort of non-mystical humanism that demands that man is the sole master of the world, that he is the draftsman of his own fortune, the chief of his own spirit.

Such idea is accepting a somewhat extreme jar at this moment. It must be admitted that if humankind is the engineer of its own fortune, it doesn't appear to make an exceptionally extraordinary accomplishment in working out its own particular fortune. No doubt the race is bombing so pitiably in working out its predetermination that it needs some assistance and direction from a Higher Power.

This disappointment of man is one reason, in the brains of Christians, for looking to such a Power for help in the emergencies of life, and at different occasions. As per the Christian view, the considerable disappointment of mankind lies exactly now. It has endeavored to get along without God. This push to get along without God is near the core of man's transgression and is to a great extent in charge of man's disappointment and hopelessness.

The humanistic push to lift up man by ousting God won't prevail with regards to commending man; it will just prevail with regards to corrupting him. Man is never noble by denying God or declining him the incomparable place in human life.

This has been attempted in numerous lives separately and on a bigger scale in networks.

God alone is the assurance of man's praise and achievement.

A few men have even proposed religion without God. Such a proposal is about as sensible as it would be for a man to welcome his companions to a dinner and make no arrangement for food to serve them.

Final Objection To Divine Providence Is Based On The Fact Of Evil In Thze World

There are two phases of this. One is the reality of wrongdoing; the other is the reality of anguish.

This protest returns into the historical backdrop of rationality. It has been expressed in synopsis form to some degree as takes after. The reality of fiendishness demonstrate that God can't be both great and all-powerful. On the off chance that he is all-powerful and does not forestall insidious, at that point he isn't great. In the event that he is great and does not avert underhanded, at that point he isn't omnipotent. In the event that he were both great and omnipotent, he would anticipate abhorrent.

We had too concede, in any case, that this issue can't be given an altogether objective arrangement.

Obvious and rundown answers for such inquiries are typically false. For a certain something, we have to recall that we can't see things totally as the Almighty does. It is altogether conceivable that there are factors going into God's administration of the world that we don't catch.

There are others that we may see into fairly however don't at all satisfactorily fathom. We should permit that there are a few things that God realizes that we don't. So far as the historical backdrop of the world is concerned, the reality are not all in. We should look out for substantially more valid for the race all in all. it is additionally obvious that the existence history of each individual is interwoven with that of the race and can be at last judged just as a piece of that history.

So far as transgression is concerned, God isn't in charge of wrongdoing. He is in charge of making the sort of world that made sin conceivable. Be that as it may, sin is chargeable to man's decision. Man isn't a mechanization. He picks insidious; and when he picks fiendish he should bear the results. It would not be an ethical world if man couldn't pick abhorrent; nor would it be an ethical world in the event that he didn't endure the results of his insidious decision.

To state, at that point, that the world is an ethical request is to avow the likelihood of wrongdoing and to assert that man must bear the outcomes of his transgression. The main way God could have ensured the avoidance of transgression and its shrewd outcomes would have been to make a non-moral world. That implies a world administered by mechanical need as opposed to by moral law.

That sort of a world couldn't in any regard mirror the integrity of God. If God somehow managed to make a world through which he could show his decency and which would incorporate animals equipped for perceiving and acknowledging moral goodness, at that point he should create an ethical world with the danger of permitting sin in it with all transgression's shrewd involve.

As to God's all-powerfulness, this does not imply that God can do anything that man can consider. A few things that we imagine are ethically preposterous and conflicting. Such an origination is the possibility of an ethical world with transgression coercively prohibited from it.

Truly, it takes a more noteworthy God to make moral request in which sin is a plausibility than it does to make a mechanical world in which sin would be inconceivable.

In addition, the Christian teaching of redemption implies that transgression costs God more than it does man. We are protected in saying, at that point, that the estimations of recovery in God's psyche and object were to such an extent that he was ready to make an ethical universe, with every one of the shades of malice specialist upon the passage of wrongdoing and good issue, that he may convey man and the ethical universe to the radiant fulfillment engaged with this reclamation.

So far as there is any objective support for enabling sin to enter our reality, it must be found in the Christian teaching of the moral law of the world, including the doctrine of redemption.

If God is justified in making an moral order, with man as a free being as its peak, at that point the issue of torment (suffering) is to some degree calmed in light of the fact that a substantial part of the misery of the world is expected straightforwardly to man's wrongdoing (sin).

In the event that we could remove from this present world's history the anguish because of man's narrow-mindedness and his ruthlessness toward his individual man, the world's history would make diverse perusing from what it does now.

With regards to the misery that can't be followed specifically to man's transgression, we have to recollect the accompanying certainties: man has discovered quite a bit of his psychological, good, and social improvement in life by endeavoring to defeat the bothers, hardships, and sufferings of life. Man has discovered quite a bit of life's train by endeavoring to wring from mother earth his sustenance and by battling the evidently threatening powers of nature.

These powers have regularly appeared to be totally paying little respect to man's most astounding qualities and have heartlessly cleared away his most exceedingly prized belonging. In any case, man has ascended by defeating these powers. As a plane must take off against the breeze, so man has been empowered to transcend the constraints of life by confronting and defeating troubles.

On a to some degree more elevated amount than this, the New Testament and Christian experience demonstrate to us that God utilizes hardships and sufferings for redemptive ends.

Providence And Redemption

To comprehend the subject of providence, we should see the world as more than a welter of clashing powers; we should consider it to be more than a moral order. To get a savvy handle of this inquiry, nothing will help us to such an extent as to see the life of man from the point of view of God's essential reason concerning man. That intention is plainly uncovered in the Bible. It runs like a brilliant string through the Bible.

The Bible isn't a book of history all things considered. The focal enthusiasm of the Bible is God's redemptive purpose. History embraces to record what has occurred in man's life and to relate these occasions in an easygoing grouping; it endeavors to follow the course of events in their causal associations.

The Bible tells something of what has occurred in human life as the events of man's life uncover God's redemptive purpose. It is concerned about these events just starting here of view. Biblical history, in this manner, leads toward, and focuses in, one individual, Jesus Christ the Redeemer of men.

Provision has time and again been translated as though it implied, particularly as identified with people, that God had his picks for whose advantage he coordinated the course of the world, and that he minded principally or only for these, slighting the interests of whatever remains of his insightful creation and maybe disregarding the request of the world to make things comfortable for these favorites.

Along these lines fortune has been translated as though God's fundamental concern was to make man comfortable as opposed to make him holy. Along these lines of taking a gander at the issue has put undue accentuation on the possibility of the parenthood of God viewed as liberal thoughtfulness and on man's comfort and ease.

The centrality of redemption in God's providential managing his people is found in Romans 8:28-29 RSV. In verse 28 Paul says that everything works for good to the those who love God, to the those who are called by his purpose.

In verse 29 he gives an explanation behind this announcement. He says: "For whom he did foreknow, he additionally pre-destinated to be conformed to the image of his Son." He grounds providence in predestination. He believes in a providential ordering of the world, because he believes in a certain kind of God. He has believes in a God of purpose and of grace. He, in this manner, has confidence that God is working out a purpose of grace in the lives of his people.

Every now and then, when individuals read the statement that all things work together for good to those that love God, they take it that the missionary (apostle) means everything work for the ease of, pleasure or comfort of God's people. When they see good individuals suffering they choose that the missionary did not get the issue right. In any case, the witness does not say that everything work for the pleasure, or ease and comfort of God's people but for their good.

Furthermore, he doesn't abandon us in question concerning what he implied by the good. He defines it in the following verse by saying that God designed that they should be conformed with the image of his Son. God designed everything that comes into the lives of his people to progress in the direction of their transformation into the spiritual image of Jesus Christ. The good that the messenger considers isn't the benefit of worldly belongings or an pleasurable or comfortable existence, But the good of spiritual character.

The most noteworthy fortunes are the fortunes of character. These are the fortunes (treasures) that Jesus Christ tells his followers to make progress toward, not the treasures that men lay up on earth and that before long pass away (Matthew 6:19). The treasures of character abide. The best thing that can happen to any man is that he be made like Jesus Christ in character. Without a doubt God could have improved a world than this to give us ease, comfort and pleasure; yet it is hard to think about any solid regard in which this world may be changed and make a better world than it is for the development of Christian character.

From the viewpoint of God's redemptive purpose, we land at the Catch 22 (a paradox) that the best world is definitely not a flawless world, however one where we should need to work to improve it, to make it better.

In thinking about the possibility of provision we ought to think about it in connection to the improvement of the kingdom of God on the planet and additionally in connection to the redemption of the person. The happening to the kingdom and the redemption of the individual are fundamentally interlinked. The salvation of each individual is a factor in the coming to the kingdom.

The kingdom comes through the saving of people. In studying God's purpose of redemption, we saw that it was not to be translated to imply that God purposed to save the person as a secluded unit, without reference to his connections in the social and historical order to which he belongs.

So we are not to interpret the idea of providence as meaning that God works for the good of the person without reference to his place in the public eye or the kingdom of God. The good of the individual is a phase of the common good of all. The whole Biblical history demonstrates that God is moving in the direction of an end that incorporates more than the good of people selected out of the mass; he is moving in the direction of a universal kingdom of good as the goal of history.

Paul demonstrates in Ephesians 1:10 that God is advancing toward the goal of heading up all things in Jesus Christ, the things in the heavens and the things on the earth.

This goal will maybe not be achieved until the point when we go pass beyond history. The goal of history is an end that rises above history. Time finds its meaning in connection to eternity.

Providence, at that point, is both general and specific. The idea of a general providence that did include the minutest undertakings and considerations of life (the cares and affairs of life) does not concur with Jesus Christ's view of God. He says that not a sparrow falls to the ground without his notice. He clothes and feeds his people (Matthew 6:26 ff.; 10:29 ff.). We can cast the all our anxiety upon him, understanding that he looks after us (I Peter 5:7 ASV).

By keeping in constant communion and fellowship with the Lord we can live above anxiety and have the peace of God to guard our hearts and our thoughts (Phil. 4:6-7 KJV).

Our evidence for the idea of a particular providence is the testimony of the individuals who seek thus to live in fellowship with God and under his control and guidance. Many who have given themselves in service to God and man have affirmed and testified that their lives were lived under the sense of a divine mission and with an awareness of divine leading.

They have testified that it was this sense of such a divine mission and divine leading that gave meaning and motive or purpose to their lives. Also, their lives of sacrifice and work with the results in blessing to humanity justify their claim that God called and directed them in his service. If anybody is qualified to speak regarding this subject, without a doubt they are. They have a right to be viewed as experts in this field.

Providence And Faith

What has been said will demonstrate That God's providence isn't something that works in a mechanical or essential way. Since the good that God is working out for us is the good of redemption, our acquiring that good is molded upon our faith. Redemption is not something that comes to man automatically or mechanically. Redemption is a moral and spiritual matter and is morally and spiritually conditioned. The idea of providence has been again and again exhibited as though it implied that everything that came into our lives was within itself a good freely of our demeanor toward God and his providential dealings with us.

This isn't true. Whether or not the things that come into our lives are a blessing to us relies upon how they are received. If received in the spirit of submission and trust in God, all things work together for good. Otherwise, what was proposed for our good may even end up being a curse. It is to those that love God that all things work for good, and we may securely say that all things work for good to the degree that we love God or are directed to love him by the things that come to us.

The issue may be put hence: The reason that all things work together for good to the Christian is that the Christian is one in whom the dominant motive and passion in life is love to God. Since this is the dominant power throughout everyday life, everything in life makes it grow. When one is legitimately identified with God, everything in life attracts one closer to him and makes one more like him in character. Love to God is the speculative chemistry that has the power of transmuting all the baser metals of life into the unadulterated gold of Christian character.

This demonstrates the New Testament considers all things as good within themselves. Nor does Paul say that every one of these things within and of themselves work for good. His statement suggests that it is a direct result of God that all things work for good. It may be deciphered that God works everything for good; yet whether it ought to be interpreted that way or not, that was plainly Paul's idea. The New Testament tenet was that all things about existence, even the littlest, was under his control and he guides everything for our good.

It is God that makes all things work for our good; and their being good to us is conditioned upon our faith and love toward him. At the end of the day, all else turns out to be good to us. To the degree that one comes into fellowship with God does he overcome evil and transmute it into a means for good.

Chapter Three

Prayer

THE IDEAS OF PROVIDENCE and of prayer are firmly related in religion. One isn't probably going to have faith in one in the event that he doesn't put stock in the other. One that one trusts that God practices an providential care over the lives of men, he will probably trust that God responds to the prayers of his people.

Prayer in some form is essentially universal among men. It is the declaration of man's feeling of dependence and helplessness. One researcher composed: men prayer in light of the fact that they can't keep from it. Man spontaneously calls for help in moments of peril, and in moments of exaltation he ascribes praise acclaim to the power or powers that control his destiny.

The Nature And Factors In Prayer

There are sure components or variables that go into prayer-one may call them assortments of petition. In the broadest feeling of the term, prayer is communion of the soul with God; that is, it is the cognizant active of the spirit with God; that is, it is the cognizant active of the spirit in spiritual fellowship with God. The spirit connects in thought and desire after God and normally in spoken word expresses what needs be to him.

There is likewise in this fellowship the side of holding up in a mindful and open demeanor on God for spiritual light, strength, and guidance. It is the acknowledgment of the Unseen Companion. It is taking unmistakable and conscious acknowledgment of God.

All things considered an immediate and conscious acknowledgment of God, prayer is maybe the most straightforwardly and particularly religious demonstration of which man is capable. It is an act in which the soul looks to set up close to home relations with God as the Determiner of man's fate.

One of the particular components in prayer as communion with God is reverence, adoration (Holy Love). It is the acknowledgment of the worth and worthiness of his character and gives expression to this recognition. It is the proper response of the soul in worshipful recognition of the character of God as sacred and holy love.

There enters into prayer also the component of thanksgiving. Thanksgiving is the expression of our recognition of God as the source of our blessings and an acknowledgement of the fact that God's endowments to us put us under commitments to the Giver.

In reverence, in thanksgiving, we are perceiving the value of God's character; in thanksgiving we are perceiving our indebtedness to him for his blessing to us which are an expression of his goodness of character.

A substantial component in prayer also is Confession. Confession has an extensive place in any religion that is ethical in character. As man comes to perceive God as holy, he comes likewise to perceive his own wickedness (sinfulness) and unworthiness in relation to God. Again and again we find in the Old and New Testament Scriptures this factor of confession in prayer. Actually, it is one of the most prominent factors in prayer as recorded in the Bible. It normally goes along with love of God as sacred, holy and righteous and thanksgiving to him as good and gracious. When man sees God to be holy, he considers himself to be wicked (sinful) and unworthy.

Petition is a noticeable component in prayer. It is to be feared that with numerous individuals it is about the main factor. For a some people it is by all accounts about all there is in supplication. It positively ought not be the main thing in supplication, but rather it is normally an unmistakable one. Intercession is a unique form of prayer. It is approaching God for a blessing on another person as opposed to on self. This is an extraordinary element of prayer as we have it displayed in the Bible, both by precept and example. Abraham pleading for Sodom (Gen. 18:22 ff), Moses for Israel (Ex.32:31 ff.; Deut. 9:25 ff.), Paul for the Jews (Rom. 9:1 ff; 10:1`) are outstanding examples.

The Purposes And Scope Of Prayer

It has been expressed that prayer is fellowship with God. We may solicit: What is the purpose for prayer? We may state as per this thought the primary purpose for prayer is the right change of man's relations with God. Prayer involves personal relations and changes. It is man as a person dealing with God as a person. In dealing with God man is dealing with a concealed, unseen and spiritual reality.

Prayer is a recognition of the fact that this reality is a person, not just an indifferent power or a theoretical standard. Some say God is principle. God is more than principle. He is a person. Also, prayer is direct dealing on man's part with this supreme spiritual power.

Where there is no recognition of the personality of God, there can be no prayer in the genuine feeling or true sense of the word. There might be meditation, reflection, however these are not prayer.

There can be no love, thanksgiving, requests, no personal fellowship of any kind. The supreme thing that man needs is God himself instead of something that God can give. God is himself the supreme blessing. He is man's chief need. When God gives himself he gives all else; without God nothing else meets his need.

About what should man pray? What constitutes an appropriate subject of prayer?

The appropriate response is: Anything that concerns man is a legitimate subject of prayer. This implies anything that is of concern to man is likewise of concern to God. The God and Father of our Lord Jesus Christ is keen on everything without exception that contacts the lives of his human children.

This does not imply that we can approach God for anything we need and get it. A long way from that! Be that as it may, it means that in any circumstance, confounded by any issue, we may carry ourselves with our problem to God, he will help us to take care of our concern.

Prayer isn't an exertion with respect to man to induce an unwilling God to give some good on man. Or maybe it is such a change of man's close to home relations with God as makes it possible for God to offer a blessing he wants to give. It isn't carrying a hesitant God into agreement with man's will; it is somewhat carrying man into amicability with God's will, so God can do his highest will concerning man.

This is shown in the way that the Holy Spirit makes intercession for us. The explanation behind this is we don't know how to pray as we should (Rom. 8:26-27 KJV). The Spirit makes intercession for us with groanings that can't be articulated. This intercession isn't intervention separated from our own, however it is intercession in and through us. The groanings unutterable are the groanings of the human soul had and moved by the divine Spirit. The Spirit moves us to supplicate as per the divine will and, along these lines, God answers our petitions.

Man can't pray as per divine will aside from as he prays under the tuition and guidance of the divine Spirit. At the point when man wants any good, looks for any good, achieves any good, he finds that God desired, looked for, and achieved that good with him, in him, and through him.

God steps up with regards to all good, and prayer is no exemption to the run the show. In each craving of good, in each heart longing and aching, "unuttered or expressed," God is seeking to bring to pass his will for good to men.

In prayer, man isn't endeavoring against God, but striving with God to bring to pass what God wills should be brought to pass.

We may sum up, at that point. by saying that the purpose behind prayer is that man may keep himself in fellowship with God and God can work in and through man to complete his purpose of grace in the world. It scope is universal in that anything that concerns us is a proper subject for prayer.

Objections And Difficulties
In Regard To Prayer

In Relation To The Will Of God

One inquiry frequently asked is: Does prayer change the will of God? In a wide range of routes and on a wide range of grounds usually kept up that prayer does not at all change God. Be that as it may, that it just changes man.

In any case, to answer this question effectively we would need to characterize what is implied by changing the will of God. In the event that we mean by the will of God, God's definitive purpose or plan for the universe and man, at that point we should state that supplication does not change his will. In this sense we should state that God's will (or his arrangement for man) incorporates prayer and its answer.

At the end of the day, prayer is grounded in the will of God. God included prayer and its answer in his arrangement for the world. We can implore in certainty, realizing that God planned that we ought to pray. Be that as it may, in the event that we mean the will of God an official volition on his part, at that point prayer changes the will of God.

That is, God will a few things because of man's prayer that else he would not will. When he says that it is God's will that man by supplication should change God's will. God accomplishes something in reply to prayer that he would not do if man did not pray.

The main ground whereupon this can be denied is to preclude the identity from claiming God. In the event that God is a person and has respect in his dealings with man to individual relations and good refinements, at that point he should respond to man's immediate ways to deal with him as a man. This is a similar complaint that we consider in connection to pardoning of sins. As there called attention to, to hold that God changes in light of man's spiritual approach isn't a disavowal of God's permanence.

It is basically saying that God is a person and isn't the slave of his own permanence; it is stating that God's changelessness is the unchangeableness of his character and knowledge and that he isn't fixed, unoriginal power.

Some of the time it is questioned that to state that God changes his will in reply to prayer would make God the manikin of man. It is said that it is man's business to do God's will instead of God's business to do man's will. In answer, it might be said that prayer is doing God's will. It is God's will that man ought to do. God alters himself to man as a man. He moves by his Spirit on man's heart to pray toward his will. All praying that does not go toward God's will is futile, in vain.

In Relation To God's Foreknowledge

Another period of this same trouble is with reference to God's prescience. It is some of the time said that, in the event that God foreknows all things, at that point prayer can't transform anything and, in this way, petition is futile. What is the utilization to implore, if things are as of now settled and God knows heretofore what the result will be?

In answer, it might be called attention to, in any case, this is no more a trouble with respect to prayer than it is as to God's connection to man's fellowship action in some other regard. It is essentially a period of man's connection as free and individual to God as sovereign and total.

So far as prayer is concerned in connection to God's perfect knowledge, a similar thing holds that was indicated out in respect petition in connection to the will of God, that is, God's foresight incorporates prayer as a component or factor in it. On the off chance that supplication is a component as a general rule and God foreknows all occasions, at that point God foreknows petition and its answer in connection to every other occasion in the authentic request.

In any case, God's prescience isn't inside itself causative and does not render important the occasion that is foreknown; that is, the component of opportunity or possibility isn't removed from the occasion in its being foreknown. Prayer and its answer are referred to of God as components to be assessed with respect to what God himself will do.

Jesus utilizes God's perfect knowledge as a support to men to pray as opposed to as a demoralization.

He says that, since God knows previously what our necessities are, is a purpose behind why we ought to request them to be provided (Matthew 6:8). Some of the time men say that, on the grounds that God knows in advance what our necessities are, thusly, there is no compelling reason to let him know. Be that as it may, he knows our requirements and he realizes that to stay in contact with God and to perceive and recognize our reliance on him is our main need.

Thus he has made it with the goal that our extreme need should attract us to him. All our minor needs ought to help us to remember our one chief need. Furthermore, ordinarily, all unwittingly to ourselves, we are brought to perceive our need of God through some other need that we convey to him.

In Relation To The Order Of Nature

It is said that petition can't be replied in the physical domain since this would annihilate the causal associations of the marvels of the world. This protest is made on the ground that no power outside the physical domain can work in that domain; else we would have occasions happening in the physical domain for which there were no physical predecessors or causes, and this would make science unthinkable.

Except if occasions can be controlled by their physical precursors just, at that point science can't follow the causal associations among wonders, and, in this manner, science is unthinkable.

We have met this complaint at different focuses in our dialog; so it isn't important to harp on it here finally. Every one of that should be said is that we know in encounter the physical and the profound as commonly impacting and molding each other. Else we should nullify either domain or have dualism.

What's more, as an issue of understanding, we do know the individual domain as being fundamentally connected with the sub-individual and as impacting that domain and being affected by it. All the more particularly, in the event that we have confidence in an individual God of incomparable power, we will see no trouble in permitting that he controls and coordinates occasions in the physical and in the profound domain.

In our dealings with the physical we realize that soul or identity controls matter for its own particular closures and does as such without abusing the constitution of the physical or annoying the request of the world. Substantially more would we be able to trust that a similar thing should be possible by the God in whose will the entire world request has its reality and support.

The Christian won't, obviously, anticipate that God will do anything that will abuse his basic purpose for the world.

In view of the trouble here under thought, some hold that petition is addressed just emotionally, not in the external world. That is, they hold that supplication is addressed just in its impact upon the person who implores. With a few, prayer is decreased to a type of contemplation just; a matter of reflection and goal. There is nothing of request of to a personal God. This is for all intents and purposes the pantheistic state of mind. Others go further and perceive appeal to an individual God, however would deny that it is replied aside from in the spiritual domain.

But Biblical teaching and example, as well as experience, justify us in holding that God does bring things in response to the prayers of his people. In answer to prayer, God may lift the fundamental laws of the physical universe off their hinges.

The Answer To Difficulties Practical

When all is said in done, it might be said that the best response to troubles concerning answers to petition isn't the hypothetical answer, however the useful answer of involvement.

The colossal inquiry isn't, Can God answer prayer? be that as it may, Does he answer prayer? Also, the most ideal approach to answer that is to pray. This does not imply that one can pray just to find if he answers prayer or not. In the event that he prays just to find out the response to that inquiry, he won't find it.

To see if petition is addressed or not, one must ask in the spirit of religion, not just in the spirit of logical examination or philosophical hypothesis. Thus, long as men find in encounter that God answers prayer, there is no utilization to set up theoretical troubles saying that he can't.

There is no complaint to our looking for in so far as conceivable the breaking points inside which God answers prayer, the standards administering his replying, and the technique by which he works. In any case, it is vain for us on from the earlier grounds to finish up heretofore that God can't answer prayer. Men have frequently chosen that things couldn't occur when, actually, they were occurring surrounding them. The prayer sense is one of the most profound in the idea of man; and millions have discovered that God has addressed their cry with prepared help. Insofar as man is the thing that he is in nature and constitution, he will pray. At the point when man stops praying, he will be an option that is other than man.

Conditions Of Answer To Prayer

In one sense, there is no such thing as unanswered prayer. Taking prayer in the feeling of fellowship with God, one doesn't collective with God and neglect to get a reaction from God. The simple thought of fellowship conveys with it a common movement with respect to God and man; so that, if God ought not react to man's approach, there would not be fellowship; there would be just an unsuccessful exertion on man's part to build up fellowship.

What man looks for, or should look for, in prayer isn't, as a matter of first importance, something that God may give, but God himself. So that, if there is prayer in the feeling of fellowship with God, this conveys with it the possibility of a reaction on God's part, and this reaction is God's solution to man's approach.

In this sense there is no prayer that isn't replied. Sometimes, in any case, there is an exertion on man's part to approach God without the best possible spiritual change on man's part. In that sense prayer might be unanswered.

For the most part, be that as it may, when men talk about unanswered prayer, they have reference to petitionary prayer. That is, they imply that man requests something and does not get what he requests. In this sense additionally there might be unanswered prayers. Men approach God for things they don't get. This might be because of the way that they approach God for things that God in his astuteness sees best that they ought not have. He won't give the things that would harm his children. He gives good things (Matt. 7:7-11 KJV), and we should dependably in asking submit to his intelligence regarding whether it is best that we ought to have what we request.

There are sure profound conditions, in any case, that are important to our acquiring and keeping up fellowship with God. Without these there can be no cognizant association with God. They are states of getting our petitions of God, since they are states of fellowship with God. Some of these conditions are named in the New Testament. One of them is confidence (Matt. 21:22; James 1:6 KJV). On the off chance that one supplicates in confidence, God allows his request.

This does not imply that one can request simply anything and accept, and after that get what he requests. One can't have confidence aside from as one is drawn into profound solidarity with God. This ensures two things. One is that one won't ask in opposition to God's will; man's will will be submitted to God's.

The other is that one will be under the direction of the Spirit and the Spirit does not lead us to confide in God for something that it isn't his will for us to have.

Faith as a state of effective prayer, in this manner, conveys with it two different conditions-imploring as per the will of God (1 John 5:14 KJV), and asking under the direction of the Spirit (Rom. 8:26-27 RSV). It is expressed in another path in John 14:13. We are to implore for the sake of Jesus; that is, as the individuals who live for him, the individuals who try to do his work on the planet, the individuals who speak to him.

We can just ask in his name as we live in spiritual unity with him.

In John 15:7 this musing is exhibited in another way: We are to abide in Christ and have his word abiding in us. In different spots men are encouraged to be diligent in prayer (Luke 11:5 ff.; 18:1 ff.). Be that as it may, persistence is essentially one evidence of faith. It is faith holding on in spite of delay and discouragement.

Whatever term is utilized, at that point, in naming the state of fruitful prayer, it is dependably fundamentally the same, to be specific, spiritual harmony or unity with God, surrender to his will. There must be no cognizant holding back of ourselves from God. In the event that we anticipate that he will offer himself to us, there must be simply the completest giving of ourselves to him.

Chapter Four

The Perseverance Of The Saints

THERE IS WIDE DIFFERENCE of view inside the positions of those who talk about Christian philosophy or Christian Theology on the topic of what has been known as the perseverance of the saints.

Meaning Of The Doctrine

In the first place, it should be clarified what the issue is.

The individuals who hold this principle mean by it that one who is genuinely regenerated will proceed in faith and will be at long last delivered from sin. We have officially called attention to that there are three phases in the salvation of the individual: salvation in its start in justification and regeneration; salvation in its continuation and development; and salvation in its consummation in the final and complete deliverance of the whole personality from sin.

The inquiry here includes the relation of salvation in its beginning with salvation in its consummation. If a man is regenerated, is it sure that he will be conveyed to the consummation of salvation? Is there anything in the nature of the underlying background to ensure its consummation? What do the Scriptures teach and what do observation and experience legitimize us in anticipating?

What do the individuals who hold this teaching (doctrine) (the perseverance of the saints) mean by it? They don't mean, as some of the time expressed, that a justified individual is saved in the end, regardless of what occurs after his justification. It rather implies that justification or regeneration is an exchange of such a nature, to the point that the confirmation a few things can't happen. To state that this doctrine implies that a justified man is saved regardless of whether he carries on with an existence of sin or turns into an unjust character would resemble saying that a white man will dependably be a white man regardless of whether he should swing to an Afro-American. The explanation behind confirming that a white man will dependably be a white man is that there is affirmation in the idea of things that he never will move toward becoming whatever else.

The regulation does not imply that a regenerated man will be saved whether he proceeds in faith or not; it implies rather that a regenerated man will persevere in faith. The doctrine has once in a while been presented to establish the impression that it made a difference little whether the Christian proceeded in faith so far as salvation was concerned.

Such an interpretation of the doctrine said that God held to us; so we didn't have to hold to him. Such an "Hardshell" in its nature.

It looks on God's purpose of grace as something that is done freely all things considered and spiritual conditions. "Hardshellism" is no better applied to the beginning. Salvation is by faith in its beginning, duration, and consummation. A man can no more be saved without faith in the center or toward the end of the Christian life than he can toward the beginning. It is by faith completely through.

Nor does this doctrine imply that a man after justification or regeneration by faith is then exchanged to a basis of works and that from that point on he should earn his way. It implies that he should endure in that in which he started, to be specific, confidence. It doesn't imply that something besides faith is necessary to salvation; but it means that perseverance is a quality in saving faith. The faith that does not have the nature of persistence in it is not a saving faith.

In I Peter 1:4-5 KJV we have the issue set out unquestionably. The author expresses that we are being kept for a salvation that will be uncovered in the most recent day. Be that as it may, he not just says that we are being kept for this salvation, he tells how we are being kept, to be specific, by faith. We are not kept regardless of faith; we are kept through faith. We don't keep ourselves; God keeps us. Yet, he doesn't keep us in any mechanical, non-moral or magical way. The same God who by his Spirit generated faith in our souls toward the start of the Christian life keeps that faith alive in our hearts.

In this way we can have the certainty with Paul that he began a good work in us will perfect it until the day of Jesus Christ (Phil. 1:6 KJV).

This statement of the issue clarifies that the doctrine properly conceived implies that man is free in his persevering faith. It is a corruption of this principle to state it as though it implied that man was kept without wanting to (against his will). Man is not any more saved in the end in opposed to his will than Man is not any more saved at end in opposition to his will than he is at the beginning. He starts in a faith that is free and proceeds so. If he believes one trusts that faith can be created by the Spirit in man's heart toward the beginning of the Christian life without meddling with man's freedom, there is no characteristic motivation behind why one ought not trust that the Spirit will keep alive without doing brutality to man's will. If God can beget faith in the unregenerated sinner without doing savagery to his freedom, for what reason can't God keep faith alive in the heart of the regenerated without interfering with his freedom?

Support For The Doctrine

It is apparent, from our talk up until now, that what one accepts about this doctrine will probably be determined by what he accepts about other central Christian doctrines, especially about the nature of sin and salvation. We are talking about it on the supposition that man is a heathen against God needing salvation by the grace of God.

In the event that one considers Christianity as only a decent moral framework for enhancing one's ethical condition, at that point there is barely shared opinion enough for a discourse of this inquiry. Be that as it may, even where there is discussion to man's need of salvation from sin, there are wide divergences with regards to the ruin caused by sin and how man is saved from sin.

A concise audit of a portion of these basic elements will help in help of this doctrine of the perseverance of the saints.

This doctrine is supported by the correct thought with reference to the relation of the human and divine exercises in salvation.

The New Testament instructing is that the initiative in salvation belongs to God. This is in accordance with the possibility that the Christian perseveres on the grounds that God preserves.

The life of faith in man is a creative action on God's part completely through. Salvation isn't a co-agent deal with the piece of God and man. It is God that works in us both to will and to do in bringing to pass his great joy in our salvation (Phil. 2:13 RSV).

Synergism here is a false doctrine. Salvation is not partly, but completely wholly of God. It isn't consistent to say that God does the bigger piece of the saving; he does everything. Man's faith is an receiving faith. Certainly, it is dynamic. It appropriates; it takes. Be that as it may, it takes as one who is completely wholly defenseless. It grabs the grace of God as a ravenous creature seizes food. Be that as it may, the heathen can do no more to save himself than an unfilled stomach can fulfill its own particular appetite.

Particularly in John's Gospel this life is spoken to as everlasting and enduring. We perceive the term everlasting or eternal for this situation as conveying a qualitative as opposed to a quantitative thought.

It portrays a sort of life as opposed to one that is unending in degree. It is a life of fellowship with God.

In regeneration one's ethical (moral) nature is revolutionized to the point that he persists in faith in God, and in this manner, in a life of righteousness. This is John's view in I John 3:6-9. He says that that the person who is begotten (or conceived) of God does not commit sin; that is, he doesn't carry on with a life of sin. His opportunity isn't meddled with. Be that as it may, he is given another life by faith in Jesus Christ that can't compromise with sin and that transgression can never survive.

In regeneration there is something put inside a man that will never give him a chance to rest in sin; he should battle sin until the point when it is vanquished. This isn't enslavement; it is freedom.

Nor does this imply one never commits an act of sin after he turns into a Christian; it implies rather that the general course of life is changed. John utilizes the current state that means a propensity forever, a steady demeanor. It is this new life inside that is long-lasting, imperishable in its nature that ensures steadiness in the battle on sin until the point when sin is conquered.

The fact that we are by faith brought into vital union with Christ is an assurance that the new life will persevere. He becomes our life, our everything. Because he lives, we will live also (John 14:19 KJV). Jesus Christ abides in us and we in him. Also, he that is in us is greater than he that is in the world (I John 4:4). The living Christ, to whom we are joined by faith, having justified us in his blood, will deliver us in the end from the wrath of God.

In I John 3:9 the articulation, "his seed abideth in him," may be interpreted "his offspring abides in him," (that is God). For this situation, it would imply that the new birth brings us into a life of fellowship with God; and our life of fellowship with God constitutes an moral assurance that we won't live in sin. It is somewhat the guarantee that we will conquer sin.

This doctrine is also supported by the reality of Christ's intercession for the Christian.

Just before Peter's denial of Jesus, the Master said to him: "Simon, Simon, behold, Satan asked to have you (the apostles), that he might soft you as wheat; but I made supplication for thee (the one individual), that thy faith fail not" (Luke 22:31-32 KJV).

Jesus made intercession for Simon individually, and his request for him was that his faith should not fail.

Jesus says that, while he was in the world, he kept those that the Father gave him. He so watched them that not one of them was lost, save the child of perdition (Judas Iscariot, who was never saved). Now, since he is going away, he prays the Father to keep them (John 17:11-15 KJV).

These two cases of supplication for his disciples may give us some thought of the sort of intercession which Christ is making now in the interest of his people. The ground of our security is the way that Jesus is presently living on our behalf. This is particularly communicated in the book of Hebrews: "Wherefore also he can save to the uttermost them that draw near unto God through him, seeing he ever liveth to make intercession for them" (Heb. 7:25) KJV.

The idea here is that he saves completely, to the end, in light of his living to make intercession for the individuals who to come to God through him. His intercessory work ensures the completeness of their salvation.

Paul express the prospect of the believer's security in a fairly unique manner under the possibility of the sealing of the Spirit.

After hearing and believing the gospel, we are sealed with the Holy Spirit of promise (Eph. 1:13 KJV). This sealing of the Spirit implies that the Holy Spirit staying inside us is God's guarantee or promise that our redemption will be completed in the resurrection of the body.

In the Holy Spirit we are sealed unto the day of redemption (Eph. 4:30). This is the significance of Paul's expression that God has given us the earnest of the Spirit (II Cor. 1:22; 5:5; Eph. 1:14). The word interpreted "earnest" here means pledge cash that one sets up as a forfeit to ensure that he would not go back on an agreement or exchange went into, however would complete his piece of the agreement. The Holy Spirit of promise is the Spirit dwelling in us as God's promise that we will go into the full ownership of our inheritance in the redemption of our bodies.

God pledges himself to complete our redemption. The Spirit not only witness to the fact that we are sons of God, yet in addition the way that we are heirs of God and joint heirs with Christ (Rom. 8:17 KJV). As heirs of God we anticipate the time when we will go into ownership of our full inheritance.

We have the first fruits of the Spirit; that is, the Spirit staying inside us is a beginning, an example, of fuller ownership that we are to have later on.

This gives us that groaning within ourselves, that everlasting disappointment with ourselves as we seem to be, and that excited aching, that longing for the redemption of our bodies that will consummate our salvation. We seek after more full endowments than we currently enjoy, and the Spirit within is God's guarantee that we will enter upon that more full ownership (possession). (See Romans 8:23-25).

We have certain unmistakable articulations in the New Testament that can't be clarified on any other speculation.

We can consider just a couple of the exceptional ones. Jesus says that he provides for his sheep eternal life and they will never die, and nobody will grab them out of his Father's hand (John 10:28-29). Here the unequivocal statement of Jesus that those to whom he gives endless life will never die would be hard to blend with any view that enabled a Christian to fall away and die.

Jesus says again that the person who hears his word and believes on the one who sent him has eternal life and comes not into condemnation (John 5:24). In Romans 8:35-39, after Paul counts the things that may be thought ready to isolate one from the love for God, he finishes up by saying that none of these will have the capacity to isolate us from the love for God which is in Christ Jesus our Lord. Peter says that we are kept by the power of God through faith unto a salvation ready to be uncovered in the last day (I Peter 1:5 ASV).

These passages appear to be clear to assert that God keeps those that believe in Jesus Christ and that there is no possibility of their perishing.

Chapter Five

The Development Of
The Christian Life

IT IS STANDARD TO talk about the development of the Christian life under the term sanctification. Be that as it may, as officially expressed, the overarching utilization of this term in the New Testament is to mean the commencement of the Christian life, not its development. Other than the term sanctify (or sanctification) is just a single of various terms used to mean the development of the Christian life. Therefore, we want to utilize the expression growth or development of the Christian life.

The Need Of Growth

That the new life started in recovery needs improvement would scarcely appear to require evidence. That this life is helpless of development and requirements to develop is wherever expected in the New Testament. This is appeared by a portion of the terms utilized for Christians. One of the soonest and most basic assignments for them was disciples. A follower, a learner is a student, an understudy in the school of Jesus Christ.

Becoming a Christian is enrolling in the school. One must begin in the rudimentary things and propel review by review. At that point the Christian is now and then called an soldier. When one enrolls in the military, he should experience a course of drilling and discipline before he can turn into a successful soldier.

Undeveloped Christians are called babes. Christian instructors once in a while reprimanded these babes and manifested sorrow and disappointment because they had not made development in the Christian life (I Cor. 3:1 ff; Heb. 5:12 ff.). Peter admonishes Christians to grow in grace (II Peter 3:18).

Jesus put forward the profound life as far as living and growing things. This has at times been denied by the those who have underlined the prophetically apocalyptic phase of his teaching. In any case, whatever one may say in regards to the relation of the moral and the apocalyptic elements in his teaching, our Gospels speak to him as setting forth the kingdom of God as far as growing things.

He compares the kingdom to seed sown by an agriculturist (Mark 4:1 ff.); to seed growing of itself (Mark 4:26 ff); to a little mustard seed growing into a vast tree (Mark 4:30 ff); to raise saturating a huge vessel of batter (Matt. 13:31 ff.)

These parable demonstrate that he presumably thought of the kingdom in its individual phase and in its more broad viewpoints, as a growing something. With this the whole New Testament portrayal of the Christian life is in agreement.

While relatively few have theoretically prevented the need of growth in the Christian life, yet as a functional issue it has been extraordinarily neglected in church life, particularly in those denominations that have laid emphasis on the need of conversion as a clear, cognizant affair and that have, in this manner, set awesome stress upon pubic evangelism and revivals.

Some other religious bodies have emphasized instructing and preparing to the disregard of preaching and evangelism. To get the best outcomes, the two periods of work must go together. Those have underscored evangelism have appeared on occasion to overlook that conversion was only the start of the Christian life. They have forgotten that the new convert over who is today cheering he would say and walking on the Delectable Mountains may tomorrow be a detainee in the Castle of Doubt or even floundering in the Slough of Despond. They have forgotten that old habits must regularly be vanquished and that the entire enthusiastic, scholarly, and volitional life of the convert, with all his social relations and exercises, should be brought into captivity to Christ.

The Foes To Growth

There are sure things that hinder growth. We will take a look at the contradicting powers, the powers that must be survived if any advancement is to be made in the Christian life. In some cases one is deceived by the possibility that, when he turns into a Christian, every one of his battles are over; however it would be closer reality to state that his battles are simply just begun.

The contrast between his present and his past condition isn't that he is currently put beyond the need of struggle and effort. The distinction is somewhat that now he is given a disposition that won't let him rest in sin and that makes it feasible for him to overcome it. Be that as it may, his foes are not dead and he should battle.

One period of this resistance to Christian development can be summed up in the word substance. By the tissue is implied human instinct in its corrupt attitude, out from under the domain of the Spirit. It is unsanctioned human instinct. The Christian man finds that he is presently two rather than one. There is the "old man" and the "new," the "flesh" and the "spirit," and between these there is incessant fighting.

The substance has been crucified, however it must be executed day by day. This must be done until the point when the life on earth is over. The flesh can't be executed once for all with the goal that it doesn't should be done once more. What's more, except if the flesh is kept in subjection, there can be no advancement in the Christian life. Advancement in the Christian life relies on the defeating of those weakness and tendencies in a one's life that oppose the will of God.

This battle with the flesh will be all the harder if horrible habits have affixed themselves on the life through long periods of sinful living. Also, even where there are not awful sinful habits secured on the life, there might be egotistical and unchristian strategies for thought and action that must be conquered. These might be viewed as unchristian just as one develops in moral discernment and discrimination, and may be overcome only as one develops in character and Christian graces.

Moral discernment must be developed as well as strength of will. In all cases there are natural weaknesses and evil tendencies that must be conquered.

In any case, resistance to advance in the Christian life comes from inside as well as from without. The world sums up each one of those powers agent in human culture around us that stand opposed to will of God. The general streams of life around us set against the development of true spiritually.

Jesus did not locate an extremely suitable environment when he was on earth, and he didn't urge his followers to expect that they would. Then again, he cautioned them that they would be dealt with as he had been (Matt. 10:24 ff.). Not every person would receive them and their message (Luke 10:16). Woe unto them when all men ought to say favorable things of them (Luke 6:26). Paul says that the man who lives a godly life will suffer persecutions(II Tim. 3:12). Peter admonishes his listeners to save themselves from a crooked age (Acts 2:40). John views the world as insidious and perishing (I John 2:15-17). In any case, the Christian has inside him a power that empowers him to overcome the world (I John 4:4; 5:4-5).

This perspective of the world has frequently been viewed as excessively rigid and negative. It might be conceivable to take excessively strict a demeanor toward human culture and its activities. Surely there is nothing in the Bible to support matter is within itself insidious and that the regular accordingly is bad. It is just the manhandled, abuse of the material world and the depravity of the powers of nature that constitute the evil.

In any case, the Bible looks on humankind as a fallen race and the universe of nature as subject to vanity by virtue of man's fallen domain; and experience and history emphatically recommend that this perspective of the issue is right. To go to heaven on elegant beds of simplicity, one would need to go from a different universe than this and one of an alternate kind.

The Bible likewise recommends that the powers of evil with which the Christian needs to fight are supramundane. Moral evil is by all accounts established in evil powers that are more than human. Paul cautions us that we wrestle not against flesh and blood but rather against spiritual powers that are to strong for us within ourselves (Eph. 6:12). To win against such adversaries the Christian needs more than human help.

The Means Of Growth

By the means for growth we mean those offices and powers that contribute specifically to our headway in the Christian life. These are once in a while spoken of as means for grace. They incorporate every one of those means or offices by which we get familiar with the standards of the good news of Christ and all the more completely suitable that gospel.

They are similar means by which we are carried into saving contact with the gospel, for example, the congregation, the service, the ordinances, the Bible, prayer, individual influence and testimony.

This does not signify that any of these things inside themselves have the ability to expand the spiritual life. They no more have the ability to do that than they have the power at first to regenerate or make alive. It is the power of God alone that can regenerate or build up the regenerated life. This thought is recommended by the articulation "means of grace." These things are means by which we are enabled to appropriate to the grace of God.

Our development in the spiritual life is the same amount of a matter of grace as our justification or regeneration. We can no more influence ourselves to grow than we can make ourselves alive at first. They are equally the work of God and equally a work of grace. Paul talking about his productivity in the Christian life says: "By the grace of God I am what I am" (I Cor. 15:10 RSV).

The Condition Of Growth

The conditions of growth are the same as the conditions of entrance upon the Christian life, in particular repentance and faith; or, utilizing faith as comprehensive of repentance, we may state it is faith alone. There must be proceeded and expanding renouncement of sin and resistance to it in our lives and proceeded and increasing dependence on Christ.

Since our development in the Christian life is a work of grace on God's part, it must involve faith on our part by which we appropriate his grace. To put it another way, our development in the Christian life is the development of our faith. The expansion of faith is the development of the spiritual life inside us. This is because of the way that faith is the methods or state of our union with Christ. This does not imply that faith is the only Christian grace, yet it implies that faith is the means for our fellowship with Jesus Christ by which these different graces are created. Faith is the root guideline of the Christian life. It is the germinal grace. Out of it grow all other graces.

There must be struggle on our part against evil. Faith must not only trust and rest in the Lord; it should likewise struggle in its dispute against sin and insidiousness. There is rest of faith, yet there is also the struggle of faith. now and again made to develop spiritually than he can cause himself to grow physically; all that each of the one can do is conform to the laws of growth and he will normally develop without effort on his part.

The facts demonstrate that all Christian advancement is the work of God and that we develop by complying with the laws of growth. But, there is a contrast amongst physical and spiritual development and the laws overseeing each. What's more, one of the laws of spiritual development is that there must be struggle against evil in oneself and in his general surroundings. There must be consecrated service to God and man and striving after holiness. "Blessed are they that hunger and thirst after righteousness; for they will be filled" (Matt. 5:6 ASV). In any case, this hungering and thirsting after righteousness must be more than a passing desire; it must be the deepest passion of the soul; it must be such a passion of the soul as to control and direct the energies and activities of life.

God will provide for one all the righteousness he wants; however he must want it; must want it so as that he would fight for it, even die for it. Righteousness of character is no easily won accomplishment. The most difficult thing on the planet is to be righteous. One must be willing to swim through the flames of hellfire to accomplish it.

Be that as it may, somebody says: "Isn't Righteousness the gift of God's grace?" Yes, it is. Be that as it may, God can give only as we receive, only as we attain. The experience of regeneration is no easygoing transaction in which the soul is inactively quickened into life. It is the supreme crisis of the soul in which the soul anguishes after God and righteousness and denies forever sin and Satan. Also, the progressive sanctification of the life or growth in grace is of the same nature.

God makes the soul righteous by creating this passion for righteousness in the soul. He gives, however he gives through our effort. Our accomplishment is his bestowal. God nourishes the fowls, yet he encourages them through their efforts. God gives the rancher his collect, however he does as such through the agriculturist's planting and development of the dirt and his drudge in social occasion the reap. He gives a man an instruction, however he gives it through long stretches of work and self-denying study.

He gives the musician his expertise in winning music from his instrument, yet he does as such through examination and practice. We say thanks to him for bread which he gives by the work of mind and hand. So he gives righteousness of character, yet he gives it through struggle and effort. Faith receives what God gives, and God gives what faith achieves.

The Perfection Theory Of Growth

In various structures there has emerged in Christian history the hypothesis that man may achieve flawlessness (perfection) in this life. At times it is held this is accomplished in an great crisis. This crisis has here and there been discussed as a second work of grace. This work is spoken of as sanctification over against the first work of grace in regeneration or justification.

People are urged to look for this experience as unquestionably as they looked for the experience of regeneration. As per this hypothesis, "carnal" Christians or "babes" in Christ are in a minute made into "spiritual" Christians.

There are various genuine questioning this view. One is that it tends to create in those holding it a satisfied spirit and a pharisaical state of mind toward others. They view different Christians as "babes" and as "carnal." It is never a decent sign for one to profess to be free from sin. The closer one gets to God, the less able is he to profess to be perfect.

Once more, the individuals who hold this view more often than not bring down the standard of righteousness.

By being free from sin they frequently mean free from deliberate and conscious acts of sin (transgression). Or on the other hand they may mean by Christian perfection a heart of love toward God and a sincere purpose to serve him and do his will. They seldom go so far as to guarantee that all promptings and tendencies toward evil are removed from one's nature.

So when one comes to talk about perfection, it would be fundamental for him, first, to characterize what he means by perfection. Nearly anybody could achieve a standard of perfection that you would give him a chance to bring the standard of perfection down low enough. Any man could reach the stars in the event that he could convey the stars close enough to the earth. The individuals who hold this view utilize such words as "holiness" and "sanctify" with a decent arrangement of glibness and freedom.

This hypothesis (theory) is also amiss with reference to its perspective of Christian growth.

Christians don't achieve Christian maturity at one bound. Sin isn't totally annihilated from the idea of man at a stroke. One can't resist the opportunity to feel that the individuals who hold this view don't see as they should the radical nature of sin and don't understand its unshakable hold upon man.

This hypothesis does not concur with the teaching of the Bible. There are places where men are talked about as perfect, for example, Noah and Job (Gen. 6:9; Job 1:1).

Men were commanded to be perfect (Gen 17:1; Deut. 18:13). The word interpreted "perfect" here most likely means exemplary, free from blame, wholehearted, sincere-utilizing every one of these terms in a relative, not an absolute sense. A perfect man was a full-developed, all around created, true servant of God (See in NT I Cor. 2:6; Eph. 4:13; Phil. 3:15; Heb. 5:14; 6:1).

In a portion of these passages the Greek word is translated "perfect," in others, "full-grown." The pure in heart will see God (Matt. 5:8), and without sanctification no man shall see him (Heb. 12:14); but we are not to conclude that perfect purity of heart or perfect holiness is to be attained at one leap.

John describes the regenerated man as one who does not submit sin, but rather practices righteousness (I John 2:29; 3:6-9 KJV). This obviously does not imply that the regenerated man never commits an act of sin; significantly less does it mean that the nature or disposition to sin is totally removed in regeneration.

John utilizes here the present tense of the verb, as elsewhere, to signify a persistent or ongoing course of conduct, a fixed or settled tendency of life. Additionally, whatever he implies by "sinneth not" and "doeth no sin" he attests as valid for every regenerated man, not of Christians who have been "sanctified" in a second work of grace. In he implies by these articulations outright sinlessness, he insists, he affirms that all Christians are sinless. That would be affirming too much, even for the modern "sanctification", or the most enthusiatic "holy roller."

Also, a similar author says: "If we say that we have no sin, we hoodwink ourselves, we deceive ourselves, and the truth is not in us" (I John 1:8 ASV). Here he is obviously talking about Christians and from a Christian perspective. It is not really likely that he would affirm here that no man can profess to be free from sin, and afterward in the third chapter insist that all Christians are sinless.

Paul's statement in Philippians 3 is instructive on this point. He doesn't check that he has received or been made perfect (v. 12). He doesn't count that he has laid hold (v. 13). However, he extends forward energetically, endeavoring to lay hold of that for which Christ has laid hold of him (v. 12-14). He infers that the "perfect" or full-grown Christian is the person who recognizes his imperfection. The person who professes to be sinless therefore, claims more than Paul could claim. In any case, he doesn't in this manner show to himself a man of wisdom, but rather promotes himself as one who is inadequate in spiritual discernment.

The Goal Of Development

The objective of standard toward which we are to endeavor is nothing not as much as that of an perfect Christian character. As per the importance of the law in its spiritual content this would request that one cherish God with every one of the powers of his being and his neighbor a himself (Mark 12:29-31 KJV).

Christ himself was the epitome and disclosure of what God would have man to be. To be as is Christ, in this manner, the objective of the Christian's aspiration. Or on the other hand, as Jesus places it in Matthew 5:48, we are to endeavor to be as perfect in character as the Heavenly Father himself is perfect.

Here is a ideal that remaining parts as a steady test to higher undertaking and accomplishment in character one may climb, he finds different statures as yet transcending above him and testing him to yet more noteworthy accomplishments.

To achieve these we should accomplish more than sing, "Master, plant my feet on higher ground"; we should likewise climb.

Protestant religious philosophy has generally held that the complete purification of the soul from sin was accomplished at death when the soul passed into the presence of the Lord and viewed him in rapturous vision. While it may be hard to discover Scripture proclamations that plainly and unequivocally show this, yet it is by all accounts completely in congruity with Scripture standards and a reasonable deduction from what is taught about the soul's going into his presence at death.

So far as the complete transformation of soul and body is concerned, that is by all accounts put at the final appearing of Christ when we will see him as he is (I John 3:2 KJV). There is nothing, be that as it may, in this to forbid that we will continue growing in knowledge and character even throughout the endless ages.

Chapter Six

The Church And The Christian Life

ANY TREATMENT OF THE Christian life would be fragmented that did not give some thought to the subject of the church. In his book, Jesus and His Church, Dr. R. Newton Flew has definitively shown that the church is important to Christianity as set out in the New Testament. Dr. Flew considers the issue to a great extent from the viewpoint of the instructing of Jesus and demonstrates that the congregation was basic to the mission of Jesus as he himself set it out.

The church is likewise basic to the Christian Life as men try to carry on with that life under the conditions that we find on the planet today. The possibility of the church isn't accidental to the Christian life, however holds a basic place in that life.

One reason here isn't to set out a total precept of the church, but to indicate something of its basic nature and function in the Christian life.

The Use Of The Term In
The New Testament

No thorough (exhaustive study) investigation of the term as utilized in the New Testament is here attempted. In a couple of spots it is utilized in the Greek sense of a get together of residents, an assembly of citizens (Acts 19:32, 39, 41 KJV) and in a couple in the Old Testament feeling of the national gathering of Israel (Acts 7:38; Heb. 2:12; 12:23, far fetched). We are occupied with the utilization of it in the sense of the Christian ecclesia.

In the Christian application, it is by all accounts utilized in three detects:

1. The dominating utilization of the term is with reference to a nearby get together of Christians.

Again and again we discover the authors discussing the church at such a place, or the churches in such an area. It is superfluous here to give particular references, in light of the fact that the term is utilized so broadly in this sense and on the grounds that there is general consent such that this is the transcendent utilization of the term in the New Testament. Dr. Dana put 93 of 114 employments of the term in this class.

2. The word is by all accounts utilized in places in an institutional sense.

This is unmistakably identified with the utilization just said. Entirely, it isn't utilizing the word in an alternate sense; it is utilizing the term with reference to any church situated at wherever. This is certainly the utilization in Matthew 18:17 where Jesus is spoken to as saying: "Tell it to the church." After different methods for settling a trouble are depleted, the final resort was to put the issue before the church.

This couldn't be talked with reference to a general body, yet not with reference to a universal body. It applies to any local body wherever found. This might be the sense likewise in Matthew 16:18. This institutional (or dynamic) use in the New Testament is uncommon, and some don't permit everything.

3. The term is likewise utilized in a general or widespread sense.

This utilization is discovered predominantly, if not solely, in Paul's compositions, and by him generally in Ephesians and Colossians. It is utilized in the feeling of Christians by and large considered as an ideal spiritual body. Dr Dargan says that the word in this sense "signifies the entire group of true Christians on earth and in paradise and in all ages."

As communicated by Dr. S. D. F. Salmond, it is "the fellowship of believers regarded as an organic, spiritual unity in a living relation to Christ."

The church in this sense is regularly talked about as universal and invisible. The term general is fitting since it incorporates all believers on earth at one time, (if not every one of the holy people all things considered, on earth and in paradise). It is all universal in character, since it incorporates all believers all things considered and puts. It isn't restricted to any one class or race. The term invisible, however, is certainly not an upbeat one. Paul talks about the church in this sense as the body of Christ.

The function of the body in relation to man's soul is to generalize and make noticeable his internal life. So the congregation makes Christ visible to man. One explanation behind utilizing the term invisible is to recognize it from the church as a visible organization. In any case, the New Testament remains unaware of any general organization called a church. The only organized body discussed as a church in the New Testament is a local body, the church situated in a specific place.

The word is by all accounts utilized in the feeling of an assemblage of Christians amassing at a particular place (1) and (2) above) and in the sense of a ideal assembly composed of all Christians on earth at any particular time (3) above).

The Nature Of The Church

We may next consider quickly something of the nature of the church. What sort of an establishment is the Christian church? Here we will utilize the term mainly with reference to a local assembly of Christians, the only use of the term as connected to an organization.

1. Christianity is fundamentally ethical, personal, and spiritual rather than lawful and institutional.

The inquiry with regards to the nature and function of the church is not a superficial or surface matter as some assume. It is rooted in nature of Christianity itself. Furthermore, Christianity is personal as opposed to institutional. Schleiermacher expressed the difference between (Roman) Catholicism and Protestantism on this point to be: that in the Catholic view one came to Christ through the church, while in the Protestantism one came to the church through Christ.

In the Catholic view (Roman, Orthodox, and Anglican) Christ established an organization and to this foundation (and its authorities, particularly, the bishops and priests) he gave his power. The church, accordingly, is his authoritative delegate on earth and men come to him through the mediating activity of the church and her ministry.

The church, then, is an authoritative institution representing Christ and mediating his redeeming quality and movement to men. Then again is the view that the church is a relationship of people who have come to know Christ by an act of faith that is spiritually prompt in its nature. By spiritually prompt we imply that it isn't dependent on any official or authoritative action of priest, minister or church. For the act of faith that binds the spirit in spiritual union with Christ, one is dependent on others for a knowledge of gospel truth and for such personal and spiritual influences as will help him to receive the truth of the gospel. He is also dependent on the enlightening and enabling power of the Divine Holy Spirit working in his heart.

Such organization of the Spirit isn't dependent on a "authoritative" ministry or church. It is the immediate dealing of God with the individual soul. Indeed, if a man a thousand miles from any cleric, clergyman, or church should read a New Testament or a gospel message and in his soul turn to Christ, he would be saved as certainly as he would in a church, or in a religious service with clergymen preaching sermons or priests administering "sacraments."

Dr. E. Y. Mullins set out clearly as the chief distinction of the Baptist view of religion the competency of the soul under God in religion. The soul by virtue of its moral and spiritual constitution is capable for receiving the grace of God and of having fellowship with God in Christ, and that without the intervention of any ecclesiastical or priestly authority.

Christ in his saving work expelled the need for any such mediator. There is one middle person amongst God and man, and one is sufficient. The Catholic origination that the intervention of the church or the priesthood is fundamental in the soul's relation to God infers that the meditation of Christ is inadequate. The book of Hebrews plainly encourages that Christ is an all-adequate priest and his mediation is final in its efficiency. The Catholic conception rather makes Christ the chief among numerous mediators between God and man.

The facts confirm that in Protestantism there is the possibility of the priesthood of all believers. Be that as it may, believers are not mediators in a similar sense that Christ is nor is their priesthood to fill out an inadequate work on his part. The intercession of believers is simply personal and spiritual. It relies upon spiritual character and fellowship with God, not on official position or ecclesiastical standing.

The laying of a priest's hands on a man's head has no weight with God. Such things have a place in the domain of ecclesiastical red tape instead of in the domain of spiritual power.

2. What we have said in regards to the nature of Christianity decides to a great extent the nature of the church.

It confirms that the church is a spiritual body. A man can't of right be a member of an organized local church who isn't initial a member of one universal spiritual body of Christ. One becomes a member of that universal spiritual body of Christ by the new birth, and this new birth is an absolute to prerequisite to membership in an organized church. This isn't implied as a push to settle the relation in the New Testament between the Church as the universal spiritual body of Christ and the church as a local body more or less definitely organized. We do intend to state that no individual can be an member of the body of Christ, in either the universal or the local sense, without being renewed by the Spirit of God. This is the essential and basic condition.

One might be considered a member of an organization called a church, but he cannot be a member of the body of Christ. The body of Christ is an spiritual body. The bond that ties the members to each other isn't an external bond or external obligation of organization; it is a living bond of spiritual fellowship. It's anything but a bound of belief, nor one of effort to advance human welfare or social action. These are auxiliary. It is first of all a bond of spiritual union and fellowship with the living Christ.

All else must grow out of and express that bond of fellowship with him. A man must have a place with Christ first and to the church as a result of belonging to him. A Christian's essential relationship is to Christ; all else follows from that. The church is primary a fellowship and organization is secondary. That fellowship is first with Christ, then with other Christians. Their fellowship with each other results from their fellowship with Christ. The organization of the church is to express and build up (develop) its fellowship.

Something else that follows from the nature of Christianity, as set out already in this discussion, is that membership in the church is voluntary.

The voluntary guideline is essential and fundamental in Christianity completely through. Becoming a Christian comes by hearing the gospel and voluntarily accepting it. We may simply say by accepting it, for accepting the gospel is always voluntary. It can be no other way. There is no such thing as a "sacramental" communication of grace.

Baptism and the Lord's Supper are not sacraments in the authentic sense of the term sacrament. They pass on no grace. They are acts of obedience and show the faith by which we appropriate grace and along these lines strengthen the awareness of grace in the believer. Be that as it may, they are acts of obedience with respect to a believer, who has already been drawn into a living union with Christ in the act of believing, carrying the gospel to others so that they may believe and accept Christ.

Be that as it may, as external acts, they are to be obviously recognized from the internal act of faith which is simply a spiritual act or attitude; and, as effectively expressed, a voluntary matter. This act of faith brings one into the hover of the spiritual fellowship of believers. However, so far as an organized body is concerned, membership in such a body must be a voluntary act.

Since the intentional rule or guideline is basic, there can be no such thing as newborn child church membership. Nor can there be anything as the administration of the laws to babies or any other people who have not willfully submitted to the gospel. Such a performance is not the administration of a Christian ordinance; it is the importation of a remote component into the Christian order.

In like manner all administration in the Christian church must be voluntary. Any administration that isn't voluntarily performed isn't Christian in spirit.

The nature of Christianity as set forward above means also that the church is a democracy.

Democracy is a form of government; yet it is more than that. It is a spirit; it is an emphasis on personality. It may be more exact to state that it is an order of things that grow out of an acknowledgment of the value of personality. We endeavored to set out in going before proclamations that Christianity is essentially personal rather than institutional.

When Jesus told his disciples that the sabbath was made for man, not man for the sabbath, he was perceiving the value of human personality. That principle runs completely through the Christian order of things. Wherever any organization or institution is exalted above human welfare, that institution or organization progresses toward becoming in that regard hostile to Christians, Anti-Christian.

At the very heart of Christianity is the principle that human persons were so dear in the sight of God that he paid an infinite price for their redemption.

Democracy works on the voluntary premise. Moreover, the spiritual democracy seen in churches of the New Testament order operates for the development of spiritual persons. Sometimes the objection is made against a democratic organization of the church that lacks efficiency.

Efficiency for what? More than likely the objector is considering efficiency spoke to in a business partnership or administrative department. Chuches ought to take a stab at efficiency, however for efficiency of a different order. The effectiveness that a church ought to make progress toward is efficiency in developing Christlike character. This sort of efficiency can be accomplished all in all on a voluntary premise.

Many times church efficiency is thought of in money related terms. Frequently some kind of organization other than the democratic based would extort more cash from people than the democratic and voluntary strategy would. In any case, such a standard for measuring spiritual achievement is quite superficial. Spiritual efficiency is measured as far as character, not cash; regarding men, not things. Men are developed based on voluntary action, not of enslaved work.

The democratic principle is likewise involved with the fact that our primary relationship is to Christ, not to men. Every Christian is straightforwardly responsible to Christ as Lord and Master. Give no man a chance to set out to interfere with the believer and his Lord. Each one of us will give account of himself to the Lord (Rom. 14:9-12 KJV),not to bishop, not to minister, the pastor, nor the priest. Under the watchful eye of the Judge of all the earth, men remain on a common level. A same truth is engaged with the doctrine of salvation by grace.

Nothing brings men down to a common level like the guilt of universal sin and the grace of God that saves from sin. There are no privileged nor aristocrats in the presence of a holy God who saves sinners as a matter of grace. No form of church life is consistent with the doctrine of salvation by grace except one that is democratic in spirit and principle.

The Function Of The Church

The nature and function of the church are closely related thoughts. What we have said in regards to the nature of the church (as related to the nature of Christianity) will to a great extent figure out what we will hold with reference to the function of the church. Function is determined by nature.

We may get at the question of the function of the church by considering it in relation to Jesus Christ as head and Lord.

1. The church is the body of Christ

As officially expressed, the church is the body of Christ. He is its internal life. Without his abiding presence a organization of people may be a religious organization but couldn't be a Christian church.

The function of the church is to epitomize the life of Christ and to show that life to men. Christ is the light of the world (John 8:12; 9:5), however so are his people the light of the world (Matt. 5:14). They are the salt of the earth (Matt. 5:13). They are the salt of the earth since he dwells in them as the Savior of their lives. He changes them with the goal that they sparkle as lights in an obscured world (Eph. 5:7 ff.). Christ is currently invisible to the world; however he sends his Spirit to his people and living in them he convicts the world of its transgression (sin) and shows himself as the Savior of the world.

He is the head of the body, the church (Eph. 1:22; 4:15; 5:23; Col. 1:18). It is the matter of the body to obey the head, to do the orders of the head. The church is to be faithful and obedient to him as head and Lord.

In order that the church may perform its function in relation to him, it must be filled up with the divine Spirit. In I Corinthians chapters 12-14, Paul talks about spiritual blessings (gifts) in relation to the church as the body of Christ. He demonstrates that each gift bestowed on any member ought to be utilized for the unification and upbuilding of the body.

There are implications that even spiritual gifts might be utilized for selfish closures thus as to acquire diversion and division in the body. Each gift, the messenger (apostle) insists, ought to be utilized for the upbuilding of the body, not for individual show or glorification.

2. The church and the Spirit

The church can't complete its function of manifesting Christ except as the church is filled with the Spirit of God. The Spirit possesses each individual member, yet the Spirit's work in the body is more than his work in the individual members. His work is likewise to bring the individual members into a spiritual unity.

The Spirit is the co-ordinating, binding together, unifying power of the body. More than that, the Spirit is the constitutive factor in the life of the church. The church (any local body of Christ) is more than a society of Christians united together to achieve practical Christian endeavor. The church is more than that. It is an organization of Christian individuals formed into a unity of cooperation in Christ by the same power that made them Christians, the power of God. The Christian's primary relationship is to Christ, not to his kindred Christians.

3. The primary function of the church

The main business of a congregation isn't evangelism, nor missions, nor kindness or benevolence; it is worship. The love of God in Christ ought to be at the focal point of all else that the congregation does. It is the origin of all the movement of the church. Butt, it ought not be worship for the purpose of looking after activity.

All things considered the worship winds up secondary and movement the essential thing. God ought to be worshiped for his own sake, not for what he may improve in any situation for us. Worship is man's acknowledgment of the worth of God, not for man's sake, but rather for God's sake.

Present day Christianity up and down the line has been excessively inclined, making it impossible to subordinate God to man. Our places of worship have been displayed on the example if a business partnership, sorted out for business productivity. The voice of God has been lost in the bang of apparatus and the clamor of association.

The cutting edge church has sold its spirit for efficiency. We go to church to hear a "hard worker" in the pulpit rally the powers to put over a program as opposed to tune in to the voice of God addressing us about eternal realities. Our religious theological schools prepare men to be church chairmen, adiminstors as opposed to evangelists of the Word. The apostles offered themselves to prayer and the ministry of the word;

the modern minister offers himself to advisory group gatherings and church dinners.

Subsequently, the hearers of the apostles shouted out: What will we do to be saved? Our church members today say to themselves: how many more minutes must I tune in before I can get out and begin accomplishing something? The church loses its secondary aims in losing the primary one. While worshiping God in the Spirit is returned to the centere, different things will fall into their rightful place.

When the house of God turns into the house of prayer, it turns into where lives are changed. Paul demonstrates that when an unbeliever comes into a church overwhelmed by the Spirit, the privileged secrets of his heart will be made manifest (to him) and he will tumble down and worship God (I Cor. 14:25 KJV).

When we say that worship is the principal business of the church, we should utilize the word worship in the broadest sense. Worship incorporates the active of the spirit because of God's disclosure of himself to us in Christ. It incorporates song, Scripture reading, giving, sermon, the ordinances-each phase of individual and corporate outgo of the soul to God in Christ in light of his grace. It is such a response of the soul as cleanses from sin and brings the soul into a deeper, more spiritual fellowship with God.

The life begotten in regeneration is developed in worship. The whole life and organization of a church should spring from worship, center in worship, and end in worship.

Much present day preaching flops right here. Such ministers has for its end some quick down to earth need of the congregation or the network or some segment of the population. The evangelist may pride himself on the way that he is practical. He doesn't get up in the clouds; he stays close to the earth. However, customarily such preaching is practical to the point that it isn't practical.

To produce abiding results the minister's spiritual life must be grounded in the eternal realities of the gospel and his spiritual vision must go past the bread and spread needs of his members. Except if a church is in excess of a social welfare club, it's anything but a church. Furthermore, except if it is in excess of a teacher or evangelistic culture, it will lose its effectiveness in missions and evangelism.

A church is fundamentally a congregation of people who have been bound to God in an experience of redeeming, saving grace in Christ, welded into a unity by the Holy Spirit, worshiping God and developing in fellowship with one another in Christ.

The Results Of Worship

Such an assembly will, as is normally done, participate in practical Christian activity. In any case, it won't be such activity that establishes them a church. Their first obligation is to be a church, and a church is basically a worshiping body. Worship is the main business of such a body and the most characteristic (yet not really most self-evident) expression of its life.

Worship is likewise the inspiration of all else that the church does as a church. Worship is the first business of the life of the church.

Fellowship with God results in fellowship among men. As men worship God they are united in fellowship with each other. Typical church life prompts the development of the spiritual life in every one of the members. All things should lead to edification.

New Testament Christians were urged to practice a loving care over one another for the building up of the individual members and of the whole body. Discipline ought to be practiced in a productive way and if necessary of a punitive nature.

Preaching the gospel to the individuals who have not heard or accepted it is also a normal expression of church life. Worship toward God leads to service toward man, and the primary service toward the world for the church is to bring man into contact with the gospel. A non-missionary church is certainly not a true church. The true Christians soul is the soul of communication.

The spirit of communication will communicate in each realm of life. The Christian spirit is always the spirit of sharing. No obvious Christian can rest inasmuch as any phase of life in himself or the world in which he lives is out from under the control of the Holy Spirit of God.

Bibliography

Flew, R. N. (1943) Jesus And His Church. New York, NY.: Abingdon Press

Dana, H. E. (1944) A Manuel Of Ecclesiology. Plymouth, MN.: Central Seminary Press

Schelermacher, F. (2011) The Christian Faith. New York, NY.: London, UK.: T&T Clark LTD

Beecher, W. J. (2002) The Prophets And The Promise. Eugene, OR.: Wipf & Stock Publishers

Johnson, E. E. (2018) Ecclesiology In The New Testament. New York, NY.: Abingdon Press

Ferre, N. F. S. (1947) Evil And The Christian Faith. New York, NY.: Harper & Brothers

Ferre, N, F. S. (1942) The Christian Faith. New York, NY.: London, UK.: Harper & Brothers Publishers

Dargan, E. C. (2009) Ecclesiology: A Study Of The Churches. Louisville, KY.: Bibliolife, Bibliobazaar

The Holy Bible (1964) Authorized King James Version. Chicago, Ill.: J. G. Ferguson

The Holy Bible (1853) The Revised Standard Version. Nashville, TN.: Thomas Nelson & Sons (Used By Permission)

The Holy Bible (1901) The American Standard Version. Nashville, TN.: Thomas Nelson (Used By Permission)

The Holy Bible (1959) The Berkeley Version. Grand Rapids, MI.: Zondervan (Used By Permission)

About The Author

THE REVEREND DR. JOHN Thomas Wylie is one who has dedicated his life to the work of God's Service, the service of others; and being a powerful witness for the Gospel of Our Lord and Savior Jesus Christ. Dr. Wylie was called into the Gospel Ministry June 1979, whereby in that same year he entered The American Baptist College of the American Baptist Theological Seminary, Nashville, Tennessee.

As a young Seminarian, he read every book available to him that would help him better his understanding of God as well as God's plan of Salvation and the Christian Faith. He made a commitment as a promising student that he would inspire others as God inspires him. He understood early in his ministry that we live in times where people question not only who God is; but whether miracles are real, whether or not man can make a change, and who the enemy is or if the enemy truly exists.

Dr. Wylie carried out his commitment to God, which has been one of excellence which led to his earning his Bachelors of Arts in Bible/Theology/Pastoral Studies. Faithful and obedient to the call of God, he continued to matriculate in his studies earning his Masters of Ministry from Emmanuel Bible College, Nashville, Tennessee & Emmanuel Bible College, Rossville, Georgia. Still, inspired to please the Lord and do that which is well – pleasing in the Lord's sight, Dr. Wylie recently on March 2006, completed his Masters of Education degree with a concentration in Instructional Technology earned at The American Intercontinental University, Holloman Estates, Illinois. Dr. Wylie also previous to this, earned his Education Specialist Degree from Jones International University, Centennial, Colorado and his Doctorate of Theology from The Holy Trinity College and Seminary, St. Petersburg, Florida.

Dr. Wylie has served in the capacity of pastor at two congregations in Middle Tennessee and Southern Tennessee, as well as served as an

Evangelistic Preacher, Teacher, Chaplain, Christian Educator, and finally a published author, writer of many great inspirational Christian Publications such as his first publication: *"Only*

One God: Who Is He?" – published August 2002 via formally 1st books library (which is now AuthorHouse Book Publishers located in Bloomington, Indiana & Milton Keynes, United Kingdom) which caught the attention of *The Atlanta Journal Constitution Newspaper.*

Dr. Wylie is happily married to Angel G. Wylie, a retired Dekalb Elementary School teacher who loves to work with the very young children and who always encourages her husband to move forward in the Name of Jesus Christ. They have Four children, 11 grand-children and one great-grandson of whom they are very proud. Both Dr. Wylie and Angela Wylie serve as members of the Salem Baptist Church, located in Lilburn, Georgia, where the Reverend Dr. Richard B. Haynes is Senior pastor.

Dr. Wylie has stated of his wife: "she knows the charm and beauty of sincerity, goodness, and purity through Jesus Christ. Yes, she is a Christian and realizes the true meaning of loveliness as the reflection as her life of holy living gives new meaning, hope, and purpose to that of her husband, her children, others may say of her, "Behold the handmaiden of the Lord." A Servant of Jesus Christ!

About The Book

In this publication, "A Doctrine On The Christian Life," I planned to cover this field of Christian Doctrine. I perceive the treatment is lacking. The idea of the subject blocks ampleness. Who could give a satisfactory treatment to such a teaching? One ventures the supposition that the greater part of the adjustments in religious philosophy (Christian Theology) are the correct way.

Men are turning their contemplations toward the need and the reality of disclosure, of man's wrongdoing (sin) and vulnerability, of both the individual and social disappointment of man without God, of the ampleness of God's grace for man's need, and of the sureness of Jesus Christ and his saving work for mankind's history.

Man does not live by bread alone. It is more critical that man have something to live for than that he have something to live on; and existence without God isn't genuine life. Today, Modern man needs to confront that reality and acknowledge it.

Reverend Dr. John Thomas Wylie

Printed in the United States
By Bookmasters